MW01487072

DYSLEXIC RENEGADE

LEIA SCHWARTZ

AuthorHouse™
1663 Liberty Drive
Bloomington, IN 47403
www.authorhouse.com
Phone: 1 (800) 839-8640

© 2015 Leia Schwartz. All rights reserved.

No part of this book may be reproduced, stored in a retrieval system,
or transmitted by any means without the written permission of the author.

Published by AuthorHouse 06/29/2017

ISBN: 978-1-4969-7001-5 (sc)
ISBN: 978-1-4969-7002-2 (e)

Library of Congress Control Number: 2015902391

Print information available on the last page.

This book is printed on acid-free paper.

Because of the dynamic nature of the Internet, any web addresses or
links contained in this book may have changed since publication and
may no longer be valid. The views expressed in this work are solely those
of the author and do not necessarily reflect the views of the publisher,
and the publisher hereby disclaims any responsibility for them.

**Experience dyslexia
through a 9 year old girl's eyes!**

I used to like school but then I started to not do so well in school. I tried really hard and I did all my homework and classwork.

I was failing all my tests. I didn't like getting them back because everyone did better than me. People were telling me that I am really smart and bright but I did not feel so smart and bright. I hated bringing home my failing tests because it showed I really was not smart and bright.

I cried. I couldn't understand why I was failing. That made me feel upset and like I couldn't do anything right. Have you ever felt like this? I know some people feel like this but I feel like this all the time.

My parents went to my school and talked to my teachers and my teachers said "Leia is holding her own." I wasn't sure what that meant. My parents explained that it meant I was doing OK.

So I continued to do my classwork and homework and to try my best. Homework was hard for me. I cried every time I had to do my homework. I was frustrated. My mom and dad were frustrated.

7

8

Every day after school my mom and I would talk about all the things I learned in school. I liked telling her the names of the bones we learned in science and the yucky facts about spiders. I liked telling her about dissecting the owl pellets and that bones in them tell us what owls eat. I liked telling her about the math trick for multiplying by nines. My mom liked hearing everything about my day. She said that my days sound interesting and like I'm learning a lot. I was happy and I felt smart talking to her.

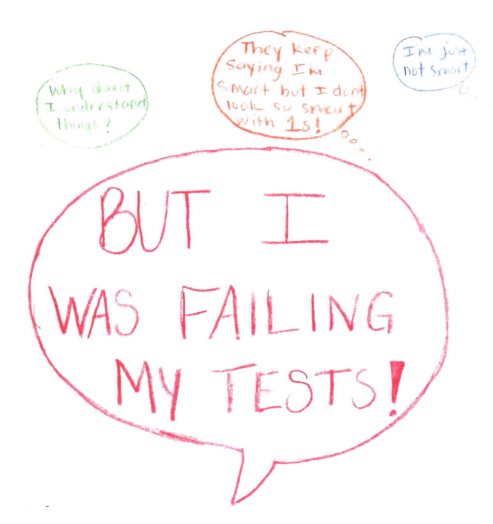

I felt not smart and bright again. I was embarrassed. I did not want to show my parents my tests but I had to. They had to sign them. They always said the same thing. They said, "Why are you so upset with a number on a piece of paper? It doesn't show how smart you really are. Let's look at what you do know!"

We would review the tests. It turns out I knew the answers and I would answer them correctly when she read the questions to me. My mom noticed I was confusing my 5s with 2s and 9s with 6s. Sometimes I would get the numbers wrong but I did know what to do with the math problems!

In reading, I would actually not read everything on the page. I would look at the first letter and then guess the word. That was my secret. I hated getting called on to read in class.

$$52 - 725 - 7$$

$$96 - 769 - 7$$

"The tac Meowed lovely when
pet by me."

My mom noticed this and took me to a doctor called a neurologist. He talked to me and had me read, write, do certain puzzles and do some exercises. He said I show signs of being dyslexic and have to go to a different doctor to tell for sure. Dyslexia sounded scary. I thought I had a scary disease.

So I went to the other doctor. I did all sorts of activities for two whole days. Some were fun and some were easy and some were hard.

I liked this doctor a lot. She was nice and understanding and explained that not everyone knows everything. She told me she wanted to see how I read, write and solve problems. She told me that I was "articulate" and I didn't know what that meant. I learned it means that I express myself very clearly. All these activities made me tired.

When we finished everything, they told me that I am dyslexic for sure. This time the word didn't scare me. This time I felt relieved that there's a reason I was having a hard time reading, spelling and doing math. They told me that many people are dyslexic, even famous people like Walt Disney, Albert Einstein and Alyssa Milano. This means that I don't have to feel not smart anymore. I just learn differently.

So reading, math, writing and spelling will always be hard for me but I will always try my best. I know with the right ways of teaching I can learn. I feel better knowing that dyslexia is a learning style! I was told that all it means is that the brain has trouble breaking words into sounds like C-A-T for "cat". Sometimes letters in words get mixed up like "pat" and "tap" and other times the words get all mishymashy and look all wrong.

I hope that everyone who reads this feels better about being dyslexic and calls it a learning style instead of a learning disability. Tell them that the Dyslexia Renegade said that!!! The Dyslexic Renegade also says that people who are dyslexic have creative superminds so use it !

Oh, and she also says you can do anything you want...if you can think it, you can do it!

I'm Leia. I'm 9 and in the fourth grade. I wrote this book because when I found out I am dyslexic I thought there was something wrong with me and there isn't. I don't want other kids to think like I did. Dys means difficulty in Greek and Lexis means words in Greek so all it really means is that a person has a hard time with anything that has to do with words but it doesn't mean we aren't smart! I also want to change a few things that I learned like dyslexia is a learning disability? Why? It should be called a learning style because that's what it is! I feel bad when others feel bad because they think they are different but really we are all different types of learners. We all need to be dyslexia renegades and help people understand what we need to be successful.

CPSIA information can be obtained
at www.ICGtesting.com
Printed in the USA
BVHW021520151118
533107BV00004B/26/P